EYEWITNESS TO HISTORY

WITHDRAWN

Inside the

LABOR
MOVEMENT

WATERMAN REPAIR

UNFAIR

LOCAL 419·A.F.L.

UNITED TEXTILE
WORKERS OF
AMERICA
AFFILIATED WITH
A.F. of L. LOCAL

Gareth Stevens
PUBLISHING

By Therese M. Shea

Please visit our website, www.garethstevens.com. For a free color catalog of all our high-quality books, call toll free 1-800-542-2595 or fax 1-877-542-2596.

Library of Congress Cataloging-in-Publication Data

Names: Shea, Therese, author.
Title: Inside the labor movement / Therese M. Shea.
Description: New York : Gareth Stevens Publishing, [2018] | Series:
  Eyewitness to history: major cultural movements | Includes index.
Identifiers: LCCN 2017018197| ISBN 9781538211618 (pbk. book) | ISBN
  9781538211625 (6 pack) | ISBN 9781538211632 (library bound book)
Subjects: LCSH: Labor movement–United States–History–Juvenile literature.
  | Labor unions–United States–History–Juvenile literature.
Classification: LCC HD8066 .S448 2018 | DDC 331.880973–dc23
LC record available at https://lccn.loc.gov/2017018197

First Edition

Published in 2018 by
Gareth Stevens Publishing
111 East 14th Street, Suite 349
New York, NY 10003

Copyright © 2018 Gareth Stevens Publishing

Designer: Katelyn E. Reynolds
Editor: Therese Shea

Photo credits: Cover, p. 1 (person) Harold M. Lambert/Lambert/Getty Images; cover, pp. 1 (background image), 11, 13 Bettmann/Getty Images; cover, p. 1 (logo quill icon) Seamartini Graphics Media/Shutterstock.com; cover, p. 1 (logo stamp) YasnaTen/ Shutterstock.com; cover, p. 1 (color grunge frame) DmitryPrudnichenko/Shutterstock.com; cover, pp. 1–32 (paper background) Nella/Shutterstock.com; cover, pp. 1–32 (decorative elements) Ozerina Anna/Shutterstock.com; pp. 1–32 (wood texture) Reinhold Leitner/Shutterstock.com; pp. 1–32 (open book background) Elena Schweitzer/ Shutterstock.com; pp. 1–32 (bookmark) Robert Adrian Hillman/Shutterstock.com; p. 5 David McNew/Getty Images; p. 7 DcoetzeeBot/Wikipedia.org; p. 9 ForestJay/ Wikipedia.org; p. 15 Interim Archives/Getty Images; p. 17 (both) Malik Shabazz/ Wikipedia.org; p. 19 Lewis Wickes Hine/Library of Congress/Corbis/VCG via Getty Images; p. 21 Central Press/Getty Images; p. 23 Carrite/Wikipedia.org; p. 25 Keystone/ Getty Images; p. 27 MPI/Getty Images.

Printed in the United States of America

CPSIA compliance information: Batch #CW18GS: For further information contact Gareth Stevens, New York, New York at 1-800-542-2595.

CONTENTS

The Good Fight.. 4

In the Beginning 6

The Industrial Revolution.............................. 8

Unions in Tough Times 12

The Haymarket Riot...................................... 16

Child Labor...18

The AFL..22

The Triangle Shirtwaist Fire.......................... 24

The Labor Movement Lives On.......................28

Glossary..30

For More Information..................................... 31

Index..32

*Words in the glossary appear in **bold** type the first time they are used in the text.*

THE GOOD
Fight

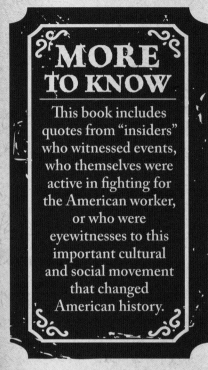
Can you imagine quitting school to get a full-time job? What if that job was working in a hot, smelly factory for 12 hours a day? You might even be forced to take on a dangerous task that could lead to a severe injury. And still, you might earn only a very small amount of money. There was a time in US history when young people, sometimes young children, had to do this.

Thankfully, many people realized that labor conditions like these were unjust. They fought for years to change laws so that children didn't have to work and adults were employed in safe workplaces. These were just two of many causes of the American labor movement, the organized campaign to improve conditions for working people.

The labor movement isn't a cause of the past. There are still people fighting for labor reforms in the United States and around the world.

LONG DAY OF LABOR

In the 1700s, most workers, whether they were farmers, factory hands, or shopkeepers, labored from sunup to sundown. This workday was hours longer in summer than in winter. In 1791, American carpenters complained about this schedule and proposed a shorter workday for themselves, *"to commence [begin] at 6 o'clock in the morning and terminate [end] at 6 in the evening of each day."* A workday less than 12 hours would have been unusual.

IN THE
Beginning

One of the earliest recorded American labor movement **tactics**—the strike—took place in 1768, before the colonies became the United States. **Journeymen** tailors in New York refused to work in order to force their employers to raise their wages.

In 1794, a group of Philadelphia shoemakers created a union called the Federal Society of Journeymen Cordwainers. (A cordwainer made shoes from leather.) This was the first organized US labor union, an organization set up to work on behalf of members' interests in the workplace. The union staged several strikes, which were then called "turn-outs." The Federal Society of Journeymen Cordwainers didn't just strike.

TACTICS ON TRIAL

Eight leaders of the Philadelphia shoemakers' union were put on trial for their tactics in 1806. In the trial, called *The Commonwealth v. George Pullis, et al.,* employer John Bedford claimed the union *"broke the window with potatoes, which had pieces of broken shoemakers' tacks in them."* Another shoemaker swore that he joined the union because the union *"threatened to [kill me]"* if he hadn't. The jury found the shoemaker union leaders guilty *"of a **conspiracy** to raise their wages."*

They also tried to prevent other shoemakers who weren't with their union from taking their places at work.

Shoemakers who did union shoemakers' jobs during a strike were called "scabs," a term that's still used today for someone who replaces a striker. This photo shows a cordwainer at work.

MORE TO KNOW

Courts often viewed labor unions unfavorably in their early days. The leaders of the Federal Society of Journeymen Cordwainers were each fined $8, which was about a week of wages.

THE INDUSTRIAL
Revolution

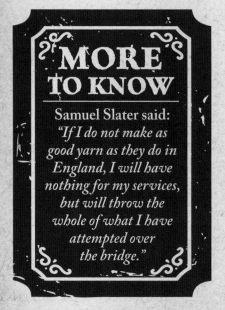
Unions popped up in cities all over the United States in the 1800s. They promoted using their own skilled labor force over cheaper unskilled workers. They also expanded, sometimes joining forces with other unions in a single city. In 1852, the National Typographical Union, largely made up of newspaper printers, organized a union of workers across the entire United States.

However, a major change swept the nation in the 19th century. The Industrial Revolution transformed the American workplace. Machines were introduced that could do the work that people once did by hand. These machines were driven by steam and, later, other forms of power, rather than by the force of people or animals. This opened the way for factories to replace skilled workers in many industries.

The Industrial Revolution began in England in the late 1700s with improved steam engines, which powered machinery, trains, and ships. The start of the American Industrial Revolution is often credited to Samuel Slater, who opened an industrial cotton mill in 1790.

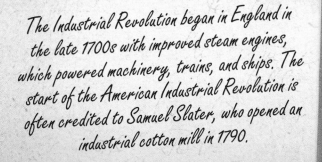

CHANGING WORKPLACES

In the late 1700s and early 1800s, a "master" was usually in charge of an American workshop. Craftsmen worked for him. In the beginning days of unions, it was the master and craftsmen who **negotiated** over conditions and wages. Later, merchant **capitalists** took a role. They supplied the workshop with materials and owned the finished products. To increase profits, they wanted craftsmen to increase output, sometimes at reduced wages. Large factories replaced most workshops in the 1800s.

The Industrial Revolution wasn't just about machines. Another major advance was the factory system. This was a manufacturing method based on producing a massive amount of goods in a large location, replacing the many small skilled workshops of the past.

In New England, thousands of young female farmworkers were hired to operate machines in factories. Business owners provided boardinghouses for them to stay in. This model was called the Lowell system.

Factories following the Fall River system hired not only women, but also men and children. Children became highly sought after because they could be paid so little. In the 1820s and 1830s, children under 16 made up between one-third and one-half of the labor force in New England.

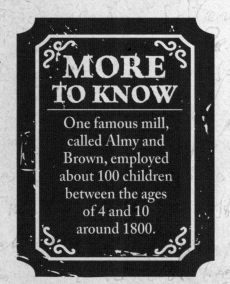

MORE TO KNOW

One famous mill, called Almy and Brown, employed about 100 children between the ages of 4 and 10 around 1800.

CONFLICTING ACCOUNTS

In 1845, the Massachusetts state legislature praised the *"neatness, cleanness, good lighting, [and] comfortable temperature"* of the boardinghouses of the Lowell system. However, the editor of the *Boston Daily Times* wrote 6 years before that *"the young girls are compelled to work in unhealthy confinement for too many hours every day . . . their food is both unhealthy and scanty [insufficient] . . . they are crowded together . . . they become pale, feeble, and finally broken."*

In Philadelphia in the 1830s, mill women made an average of $2.25 a week. Men averaged $6.75 a week. Children earned as little as 30 to 50 cents a week.

UNIONS IN
Tough Times

In 1833, a uniting of separate journeymen unions took place in New York City with the goal of working together for common concerns. Skilled workers' unions all over the United States did the same. Strikes occurred across the nation in the 1840s and 1850s as US industry boomed while wages remained low. Working conditions became worse with the outbreak of the American Civil War (1861–1865). Strikes were labeled as dangerous "civil unrest" by the government and broken up. Labor leaders were arrested.

By the end of the war, the United States was a leading industrial nation. Yet a *New York Times* survey in 1869 reported that just one-eighth of workers earned sufficient income to afford the "comforts of life" and three-quarters earned *"a meager subsistence [income] . . . their families crowded [in] slum apartments."*

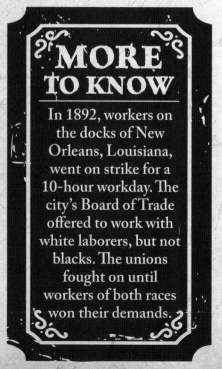

MORE TO KNOW

In 1892, workers on the docks of New Orleans, Louisiana, went on strike for a 10-hour workday. The city's Board of Trade offered to work with white laborers, but not blacks. The unions fought on until workers of both races won their demands.

A slum is a crowded city area with run-down, often unsafe housing. It's sometimes the only housing the poorest people can afford. This is a slum apartment in the 1860s.

BLACK LABOR IN THE SOUTH

Before the Civil War, black slaves worked in every kind of labor in the South. Slaves were sometimes hired out to factories because they were inexpensive and skilled. These laborers could receive wages and were sometimes treated better than those in fields. After the war, southern blacks banded together in unions, such as those for coal miners and construction workers, and later joined national unions. They achieved the greatest success when working together with whites for better conditions.

An important national labor organization called the Knights of Labor (KOL) was founded in 1869. It evolved to propose that workers' **cooperatives** should replace capitalism. The KOL became especially popular after the Great Railroad Strike of 1877 in which more than 100,000 railway workers participated and more than half the freight on US tracks came to a halt. This strike began after workers' wages were cut during a time of economic hardship. Though little was accomplished because the federal government largely sided with the rail companies, membership in the KOL swelled to 700,000 workers.

However, the KOL lost favor after 1886. This year was marked by 1,600 strikes in the United States, some violent, as well as the deadly Haymarket **Riot** in Chicago. Many blamed the KOL.

A NONUNION VICTORY

Labor reform came from nonunion efforts, too. In 1909, about 5,000 immigrant workers from 16 countries went on strike at the Pressed Steel Car Company in McKees Rock, Pennsylvania. Wages went up and down daily. *The Pittsburgh Leader* newspaper reported that when a worker was injured, a " 'boss' pushes the bleeding body aside with his foot to make room for another living man." Railway workers united with the strikers, refusing to transport strikebreakers. The strikers won their demands.

MORE TO KNOW

A Baltimore merchant explained, "The [Great Railroad Strike of 1877] . . . is a revolt of working men against low prices of labor, which have not been accomplished with corresponding low prices of food, clothing, and house rent."

The Great Railroad Strike of 1877 began on July 17, 1877, in Martinsburg, West Virginia, but spread throughout the nation, turning violent. By the time it was over, 1,000 people were jailed and around 100 had been killed.

The Haymarket RIOT

WHO WAS TO BLAME?

Eight men were sentenced to death after the riot, though the bomb-thrower was never identified. Some of the men had given speeches telling strikers to arm themselves against police. The judge stated that encouraging murder was proof enough of guilt. On November 11, 1887, four men were hanged. Another killed himself. The three remaining men were eventually pardoned after the public questioned the fairness of the trial.

On May 3, 1886, a union held a strike at the McCormick Harvest Machine Company in Chicago, Illinois, in support of a national movement for an 8-hour workday. Police officers and strikers clashed, and a striker was killed.

Labor leaders called a meeting the next day, May 4, in Haymarket Square to protest the death. An article in the *Chicago Tribune* described what happened: *"Six or eight companies of police, commanded by Inspector Bonfield, marched rapidly past the corner. . . . The reply was a bomb, which exploded as soon as it struck. The first company of police answered with a volley [of gunfire] right into the crowd."* Despite arrests and violence, the event inspired labor leaders to keep speaking out in public and fighting for fairer workplaces.

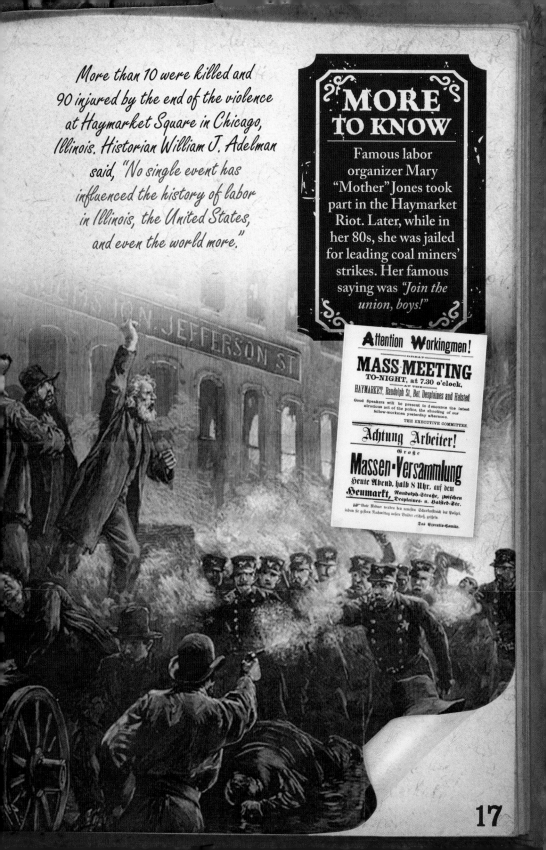

More than 10 were killed and 90 injured by the end of the violence at Haymarket Square in Chicago, Illinois. Historian William J. Adelman said, "No single event has influenced the history of labor in Illinois, the United States, and even the world more."

MORE TO KNOW

Famous labor organizer Mary "Mother" Jones took part in the Haymarket Riot. Later, while in her 80s, she was jailed for leading coal miners' strikes. Her famous saying was *"Join the union, boys!"*

Attention Workingmen!

GREAT

MASS-MEETING
TO-NIGHT, at 7.30 o'clock,
AT THE
HAYMARKET, Randolph St., Bet. Desplaines and Halsted.

Good Speakers will be present to denounce the latest atrocious act of the police, the shooting of our fellow-workmen yesterday afternoon.

THE EXECUTIVE COMMITTEE.

Achtung Arbeiter!

Große

Massen-Versammlung
Heute Abend, halb 8 Uhr, auf dem
Heumarkt, Randolph-Straße, zwischen
Desplaines- u. Halsted-Str.

Gute Redner werden den neuesten Schurkenstreich der Polizei, indem sie gestern Nachmittag unsere Brüder erschoß, geißeln.

Das Executiv-Comite.

Child *LABOR*

Child labor was one of the issues around which the labor movement gained energy. Unions were successful in persuading certain states to enact laws about child workers. In 1836, Massachusetts passed the first state child labor law, requiring children under 15 who were working in factories to attend school at least 3 months a year. In 1842, Massachusetts limited children's working hours to 10 a day, and other states passed similar laws. The next push was to establish a minimum age for child workers.

By the end of the 1880s, about 40 percent of working-class families lived in poverty, crowding into slums.

Most depended on the income of their children. This meant that children gave up school to contribute to their family.

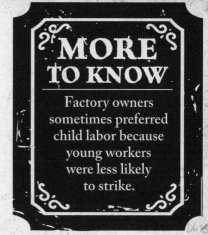
As child labor laws came into effect in northern states, factories moved to southern states with more relaxed child labor laws.

YOUNG SOCK MAKER

Bertha Miller of North Carolina recalled working in a mill at 11 years old in the early 1900s: *"I was so little that they had to build me a box to get up on to put the sock in the machine . . . When paydays come around, I drawed three dollars. That was for six days, seventy-two hours."* Though she worked 12-hour days, Miller still didn't earn enough to pay for her meals.

In 1892, the Democratic Party adopted national union recommendations to ban factory employment for children under 15 to their goals. In 1904, the National Child Labor Committee formed to begin a national campaign for federal child labor laws. Activist Jane Addams, who worked tirelessly for immigrant and working-class families in Chicago, Illinois, was a founding member.

Addams believed that *"America's future will be determined by the home and the school. The child becomes largely what he is taught; hence we must watch what we teach, and how we live."* She thought trapping children in factory work would ruin their lives and harm the whole country eventually. However, it wasn't until 1938 that federal law regulated ages of employment and work hours for children under the Fair Labor Standards Act.

Under the Fair Labor Standards Act, children under 18 cannot do certain dangerous jobs, and children under the age of 16 cannot work during school hours.

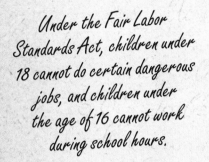

MORE TO KNOW

Jane Addams opened Hull House in Chicago for working-class families. It offered kindergarten and daycare for children, an art gallery, libraries, music and art classes, and an employment bureau.

THE AFL

In 1886, some unions organized themselves into the American Federation of Labor (AFL) under the leadership of Samuel Gompers. It was made up of about 100 national and international unions. The AFL concentrated on **collective bargaining** to decide wages, benefits, hours, and working conditions.

In the *Rocky Mountain News* in 1881, Samuel Gompers explained why he thought unions were important: *"Do I believe in **arbitration**? I do. But not in arbitration between the lion and the lamb, in which the lamb is in the morning found inside the lion. I believe in arbitration between two lions or two lambs . . . There can be arbitration only between equals. Let us organize: then we will stand on an equal footing with the employers."*

MORE TO KNOW

Labor unions thought the government shouldn't have become involved in the Pullman Strike. As a peacemaking gesture, President Grover Cleveland declared Labor Day a national holiday.

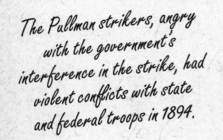

The Pullman strikers, angry with the government's interference in the strike, had violent conflicts with state and federal troops in 1894.

THE PULLMAN STRIKE

In 1894, workers at the Pullman Palace railcar company near Chicago went on strike after their wages were cut by 25 percent while the company's employee housing prices remained the same. The American Railway Union, one of the largest industrial unions, asked all union members to refuse to handle Pullman cars. Railroads in the West came to a halt. The federal government stopped the strike before an agreement was made, explaining it was harmful to interstate business.

THE TRIANGLE
Shirtwaist Fire

The union workers at the Triangle Shirtwaist Company, where women's blouses were made, went on strike in 1909. One of their complaints was that exit doors were locked to stop workers from leaving to use a bathroom or take a break. However, the workers' demands—including unlocked doors—were never met.

Two years later, a terrible fire on the top floors of the Triangle Shirtwaist Company factory in New York City brought national attention to unsafe working conditions. In just 18 minutes, 136 people died because they couldn't escape the building. Only the manager had the key. One witness said: *"I saw groups of women embracing each other and leaping to the sidewalk. The firemen were helpless."* Three months after the fire, New York enacted a state law creating the Factory Investigating Commission.

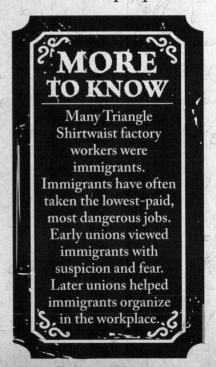

MORE TO KNOW

Many Triangle Shirtwaist factory workers were immigrants. Immigrants have often taken the lowest-paid, most dangerous jobs. Early unions viewed immigrants with suspicion and fear. Later unions helped immigrants organize in the workplace.

THE FACTORY INVESTIGATING COMMISSION

The Factory Investigating Commission created more than 30 labor laws in New York addressing fire safety and **sanitation**. The following year, the State Department of Labor was created. According to historian Richard Greenwald, the factory fire *"opened a system that was for so long seen as a private system between a worker and an owner. . . It can never be private again. There are 146 women, men who died because that was a private system."*

More than 350,000 people took part in a funeral march for the Triangle Shirtwaist Company workers who had been killed.

In the 1960s, unions played a role in battling **discrimination** against **minorities** and women in the workplace.

Union numbers dropped beginning in the 1970s as the US economy transformed. More foreign goods came into the nation, US factories moved to other countries for cheaper labor, and American plants closed. In the 1980s and 1990s, ongoing falling membership made unions join together. However, many more women, immigrants, and minorities than ever before became union members.

Historian Thomas Bender said that before the Triangle Shirtwaist fire, people *"had tolerated a kind of set of employment and other industrial practices that they should never have tolerated . . . there are things that have to be managed not by the market but by public policy."* President Franklin Roosevelt agreed with this concept.

In the 1930s, Roosevelt appointed officials from New York's Fire Factory Investigating Commission to federal government positions. These included Frances Perkins, the first female to serve in the presidential cabinet. Frances Perkins had also worked at Hull House in Chicago. She believed: *"The people are what matter to government, and a government should aim to give all the people . . . the best possible life."* Unions grew under Roosevelt's presidency.

MORE TO KNOW

In 1935, a miners' union helped form the Committee (later, Congress) for Industrial Organization, or the CIO. It became home to unions in the auto, rubber, and steel industries. The CIO joined with the AFL in 1955. The AFL-CIO is still in existence.

A cartoon shows Franklin Roosevelt signing the 1935 National Labor Relations Act with Frances Perkins behind him. The act protected the rights of employees and employers and promoted collective bargaining. By 1945, more than 12 million American workers were union members.

THE LABOR

Movement Lives On

It's not always unions guiding labor reform. Unions don't include every worker and don't include some of the lowest-paid employees. Time and time again, though, groups with common interests—union or not—have banded together to bargain for better benefits, including farmers, women, immigrants, migrant workers, college students, and others.

In 2009, an organization called the United Students Against **Sweatshops** asked 96 US colleges not to hire Russell Athletic clothing company to make school clothing. The company had closed a plant in Honduras after the workers there had tried to form a union. Under pressure, the clothing company reopened the factory and rehired all the workers. The history of US labor reflects that even the seemingly powerless can find strength when they act together—even across country borders.

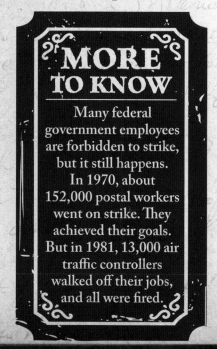

MORE TO KNOW

Many federal government employees are forbidden to strike, but it still happens. In 1970, about 152,000 postal workers went on strike. They achieved their goals. But in 1981, 13,000 air traffic controllers walked off their jobs, and all were fired.

TIMELINE

KEY MOMENTS IN THE AMERICAN LABOR MOVEMENT

1768 — One of the earliest recorded strikes takes place in the American colonies.

1790 — Samuel Slater opens the first industrial cotton mill in the United States.

1794 — Philadelphia shoemakers create a union, but are later found guilty of conspiracy.

1836 — Massachusetts passes the first state child labor law.

1869 — The national labor organization called the Knights of Labor is founded.

1877 — More than 100,000 railway workers participate in the Great Railroad Strike.

1886 — Strikers in Chicago clash with police, beginning the Haymarket Square Riot.

1894 — Union workers strike against the Pullman Palace railcar company.

1911 — A fire kills workers at the Triangle Shirtwaist Company, touching off new workplace regulations.

1935 — The National Labor Relations Act is passed, protecting the rights of employees and employers.

1938 — The Fair Labor Standards Act regulates employment for children.

1955 — The American Federation of Labor (AFL) and the Congress for Industrial Organization (CIO) unite.

1970 — About 152,000 postal workers go on strike and succeed in a wage increase.

1981 — About 13,000 members of the national union of air traffic controllers go on strike and are fired.

2009 — United Students Against Sweatshops pressures Russell Athletic clothing to reopen a Honduran factory and rehire workers.

UNION OR NO?

William Burress, former president of the American Postal Workers Union once said unions fight *"to ensure that the balance is not tipped in favor of the employer."* But some workers choose not to join unions. Union members may have to pay hundreds of dollars in yearly dues. They must strike when their union decides to do so, which can mean lost wages. They also must follow union agreements in the workplace, whether they benefit from them or not.

29

GLOSSARY

arbitration: a process of settling an argument or disagreement in which people on both sides present opinions and ideas to a third person or group

capitalist: one who believes the best economic system is capitalism, an economic system in which things used to make and transport products are owned by people and companies rather than by governments and prices are determined by competition in a free market

collective bargaining: talks between an employer and leaders of a union about wages, benefits, and other workplace conditions

conspiracy: the act of secretly planning to do something harmful or illegal

cooperative: a business or organization owned and operated by people who work there or who use its services

discrimination: the practice of unfairly treating a person or group of people differently from other people or groups of people

journeyman: a worker who learns a skill and then works for another person

minority: a group of people who are different from a larger group in a country in some way, such as race or religion

negotiate: to discuss something formally in order to make an agreement

riot: a situation in which a large group of people behave in a violent and uncontrolled way

sanitation: the process of keeping places free from dirt, infection, and disease by removing waste and garbage

sweatshop: a shop or factory in which employees work for long hours at low wages under unhealthy conditions

tactic: an action or method that is planned and used to achieve a particular goal

FOR MORE
Information

Books

Burgan, Michael. *The Pullman Strike of 1894*. Minneapolis, MN: Compass Point Books, 2008.

Otfinoski, Steven. *The Child Labor Reform Movement: An Interactive History Adventure*. North Mankato, MN: Capstone Press, 2014.

Peppas, Lynn Leslie. *Workers' Rights*. New York, NY: Crabtree Publishing Company, 2017.

Websites

A History of Child Labor
www.scholastic.com/teachers/articles/teaching-content/history-child-labor/
Find out more about child labor in America.

Labor Movement
www.history.com/topics/labor
Read a short history of unions and the labor movement.

INDEX

Addams, Jane 20, 21

American Federation of Labor 22, 27, 29

black workers 12, 13

child labor 4, 10, 11, 18, 19, 20

child labor laws 18, 19, 20, 21, 29

Committee (Congress) for Industrial Organization 27, 29

factory 4, 8, 9, 10, 13, 18, 19, 20, 24, 25, 26, 28

Fair Labor Standards Act 20, 21, 29

Gompers, Samuel 22

Great Railroad Strike of 1877 14, 15, 29

Haymarket Square Riot 14, 16, 17, 29

immigrants 14, 20, 24, 26, 28

Jones, Mary "Mother" 17

Knights of Labor 14, 29

Labor Day 22

National Labor Relations Act 27, 29

Pullman Strike 22, 23, 29

Roosevelt, Franklin 26, 27

scab 7

school 4, 18, 19, 20, 21

skilled workers 8, 10, 12, 13

slum 12, 13, 18

strike 6, 7, 12, 14, 16, 17, 19, 23, 24, 28, 29

Triangle Shirtwaist Company fire 24, 25, 26, 29

union 6, 7, 8, 9, 12, 13, 16, 17, 18, 20, 22, 23, 24, 26, 27, 28, 29

United Students Against Sweatshops 28, 29

wages 6, 7, 9, 12, 13, 14, 22, 23, 29

women 10, 11, 26, 28

workday length 4, 5, 11, 12, 16, 18, 20, 22

working conditions 4, 9, 12, 13, 22, 24